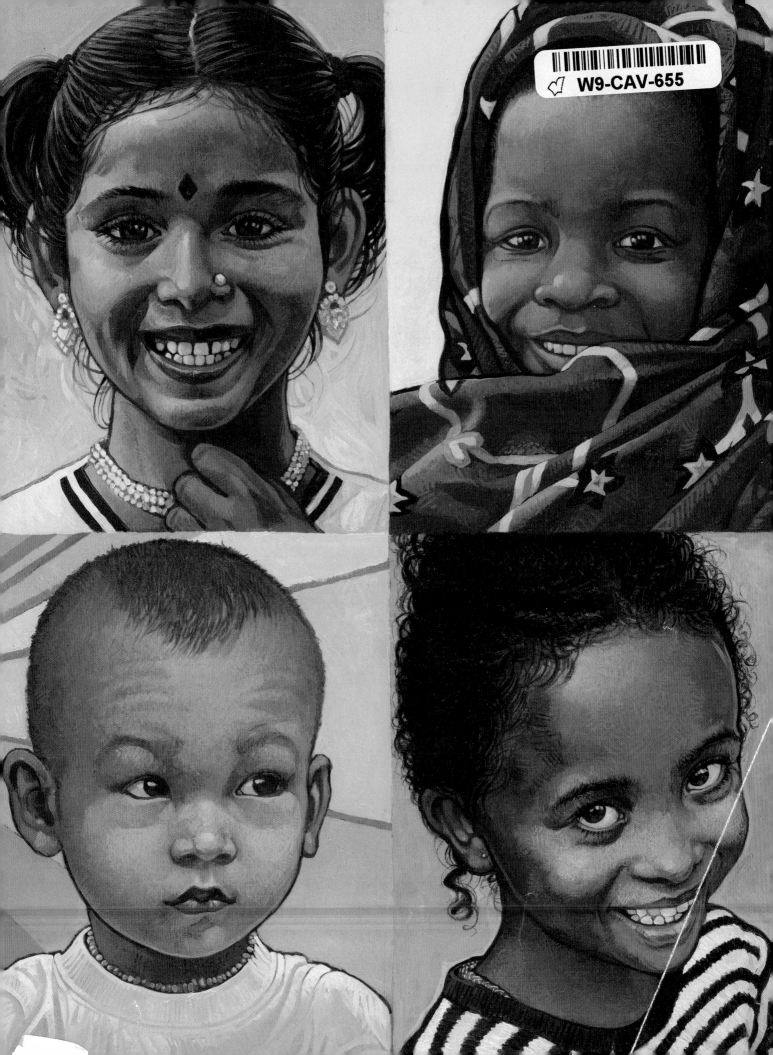

ZONDERKIDZ

The Lord's Prayer
Ancillary text copyright © 2010 by Rick Warren
Illustrations © 2010 by Richard Jesse Watson

Requests for information should be addressed to:
Zonderkidz, Grand Rapids, Michigan 49530

Library of Congress Cataloging-in-Publication Data

The Lord's Prayer / illustrated by Richard Jesse Watson
        p.   cm.
    ISBN 978-0-310-71086-8 (hardcover)
    [1. Lord's Prayer—Juvenile literature. I. Watson, Richard Jesse. II. The Lord's Prayer.
BV323.L6713 2011
226.9'6—dc22   2009037508

All Scripture quotations, unless other wise indicated, are taken from the King James Version of the Bible.

Any Internet addresses (websites, blogs, etc.) and telephone numbers printed in this book are offered as a resource. They are not intended in any way to be or imply an endorsement by Zondervan, nor does Zondervan vouch for the content of these sites and numbers for the life of this book.

Editor. Barbara Herndon
Interior & cover design: Cindy Davis

Printed in the United States of America

10 11 12 13 14 15 /WPR/ 10 9 8 7 6 5 4 3 2

*For Our Children
and
Grandchildren*

*Thank you to my family and friends
who modeled, encouraged, and prayed.*

*Special thanks to World Vision, Inc.
for generous permission to use photos
from their library as inspiration and reference.*

—R. J. W.

❧

For Kaylie, Cassi, Caleb, and Cole.

—R. W.

The Lord's Prayer

ZONDERkidz

ZONDERVAN.com/
AUTHORTRACKER
follow your favorite authors

"One generation makes known
your faithfulness to the next."
Isaiah 38:19 (Living)

Teaching children to trust God through prayer, and praying *with* them,
is not just our responsibility—it is one of life's great privileges.

We often think we teach children to pray, but actually they have much to
teach us about prayer. They often understand prayer better than adults,
which is why Jesus said, "Unless you become like little children,
you will never enter the kingdom of heaven."

What is it about the way children pray that God loves so much? First,
they don't pray to impress others. Second, they are straightforward
and unashamed of their bold requests. Third, they are simple and sincere.
Children pray about what they care about. Authenticity, simplicity, and
spontaneity are hallmarks of childlike prayer and faith.

Prayer is the key to living with hope. Jesus said that we
"should always pray and never give up." Children who pray are less
likely to be discouraged by life. That's why it's important to strengthen the hope
of children by introducing them to Jesus' model for prayer at an early age.

It is my prayer for you that reading this book with your children and
praying the Lord's Prayer together will become a meaningful bedtime ritual, a
treasured memory, and a lasting legacy that bears good fruit for generations to
come. May God bless you and the children you love.

—Rick Warren

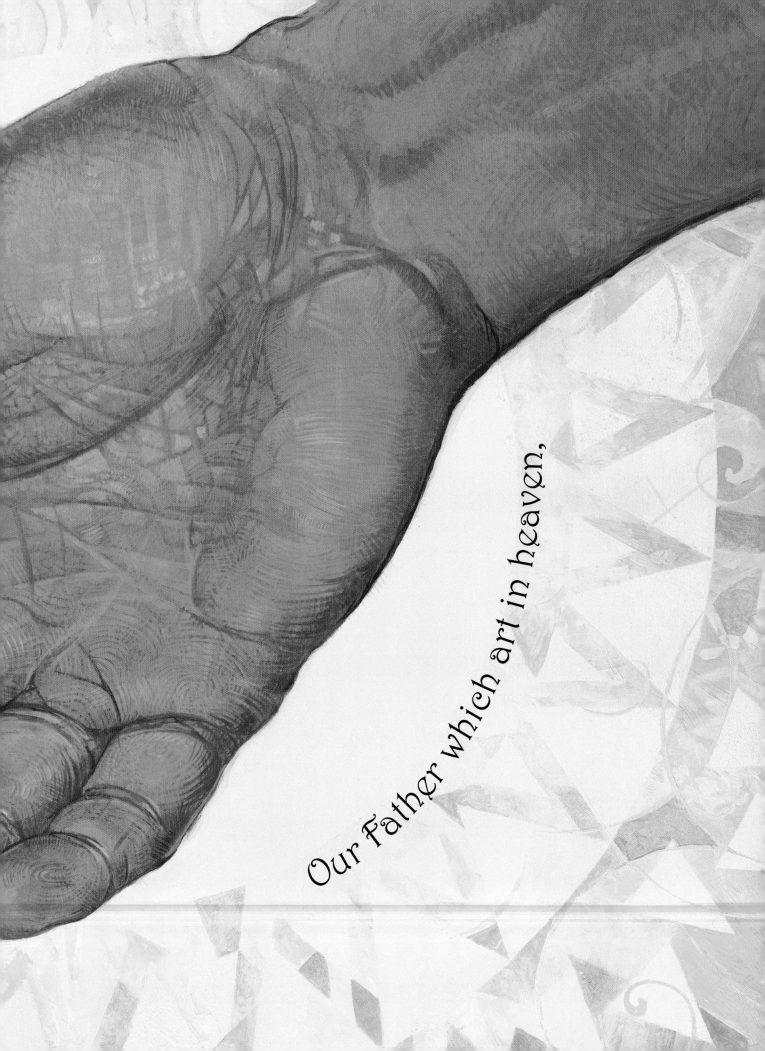

Our Father which art in heaven,

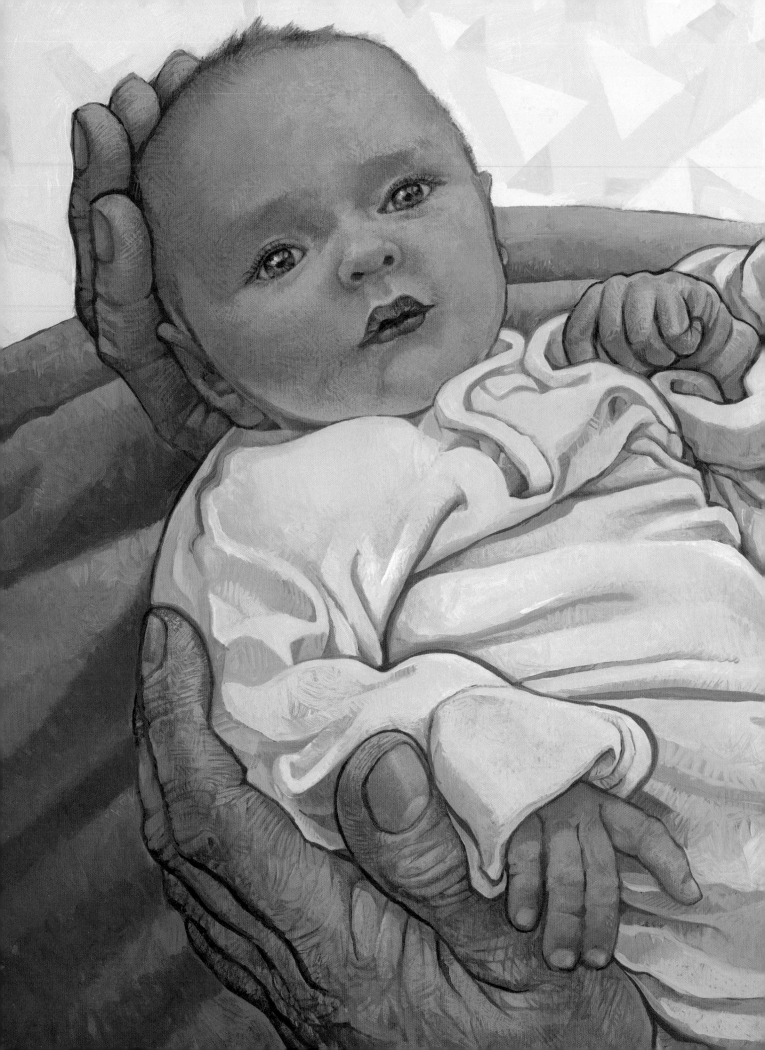

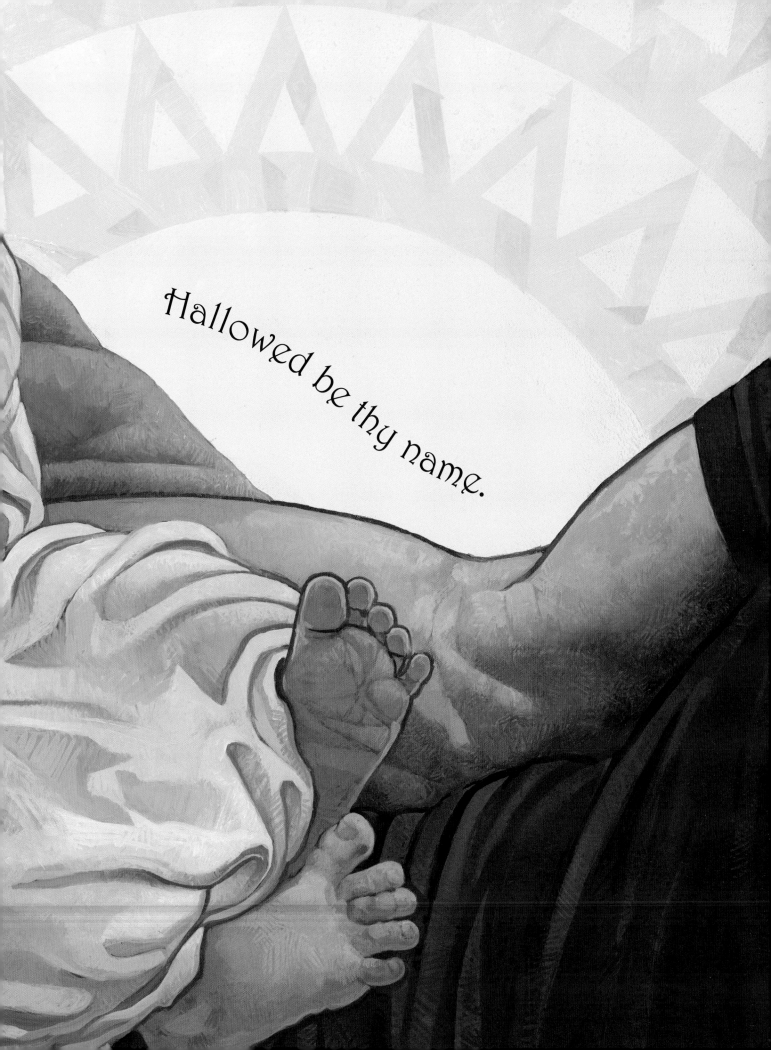

Hallowed be thy name.

Thy kingdom come.

Thy will be done in earth,

as it is in heaven.

Give us this day our daily bread.

And forgive us our debts,

as we forgive our debtors.

And lead us not into temptation, but deliver us from evil:

For thine is the kingdom,

and the power,

and the glory, for ever. Amen.

As a child, I prayed the Lord's Prayer.
Now that I am a father and grandfather,
I still pray the Lord's Prayer.

Jesus gave his disciples this prayer to show them how
to speak with God. It has been a delight to meditate on a
profound prayer that is also an interactive poem.

As an artist, I found it a great challenge to
illustrate such a pure expression of love and
worship. I experienced joy as I worked on this book. So
much so, that I sometimes felt like I could fly. My family and
friends helped me by modeling for some of the illustrations
and by their sweet encouragement.

The world desperately needs this prayer. It is about
trust, forgiveness, and a father's love.

The Lord's Prayer belongs to all the children
of the world, for it begins, "Our Father…"

—Richard Jesse Watson

Prayer is just talking to God. Even though we cannot see God, he is always near, and God loves to hear our prayers. We can talk to God anywhere, and we can talk to him about anything! Whenever we feel sad or scared or upset, we should talk to God and tell him how we feel. God always understands.

—Rick Warren

Our Father which art in heaven,

God is my Father in heaven who made me. He will always love me. He will never leave me, so I will never be lonely.
Thank you, God, for loving me!

Hallowed be thy name.

God is good to me, so I honor him. I honor God's name by loving him, trusting him, obeying him, and thanking him!
Thank you, God, for being so good to me!

Thy kingdom come.

When I do what God wants me to do, he is the King of my heart, and I am filled with joy!

Thank you, God, for being great!

Thy will be done in earth,

God made me for a purpose. He has a good plan for my life, so I am not afraid.

Thank you, God, for your plan!

as it is in heaven.

Heaven is the happy place where God lives. One day I'll get to live there too, because I love and trust in Jesus, God's Son.

Thank you, God, for heaven!

Give us this day our daily bread.

God has promised to take care of all my needs, so I will trust him and not worry.

Thank you, God, for your gifts!

And forgive us our debts, as we forgive our debtors.

When I make mistakes, God always forgives me. So when other people make mistakes or hurt me, I forgive them too!

Thank you, God, for forgiving me!

And lead us not into temptation, but deliver us from evil:

God helps me to do what is right and good. And he helps me to not do what is wrong. I can ask God for help any time!

Thank you, God, for protecting me!

For thine is the kingdom,

I am a part of God's family, which will last forever and ever!

I trust in you, God!

and the power,

When I am tired, I can ask God for energy and strength!

God, please make me strong!

and the glory, for ever. Amen.

When I trust God completely, it makes him smile!

I love you, God!

Our Father which art in heaven,
Hallowed be thy name.
Thy kingdom come. Thy will be done
in earth, as it is in heaven. Give us this day
our daily bread. And forgive us our debts,
as we forgive our debtors.
And lead us not into temptation,
but deliver us from evil:
For thine is the kingdom, and the power,
and the glory, for ever.
Amen.